EASY POSITION TUNES FOR VIOLA

NEIL MACKAY

3rd POSITION

The D string

Play the D string tetrachord and pause on the note G with the 3rd finger. Move the han
up to 3rd position so that the same note is played by the 1st finger.

1······ = keep the finger on the string.

∧ or ∨ = semitone between the notes.

simile = continue in the same manner.

TÊTE-A-TÊTE

THE SPINNING WHEEL

© Oxford University Press 1965

Printed in Great Britain

OXFORD UNIVERSITY PRESS, MUSIC DEPARTMENT, GREAT CLARENDON STREET, OXFORD OX2 6DP

The G string

The G string fingering is the same as that used on the D string.

THE MILITIA

Allegro risoluto

A LAKESIDE VIEW

Andantino

The G and D strings

Play the G string tetrachord followed by that of the D string and the result is the SCALE OF C MAJOR.

Practise also with 2 and 4 notes per bow.

C major arpeggio

1═ means 1st finger covering two strings at the same time.
Practise also using a bow to each bar.

THE COURTIER'S DANCE

The staccato quavers should be played off the string in the L.H. part of the bow.

Allegretto grazioso

BUGLE PARADE

Allegro moderato

Easy Position Tunes for Viola

The A string

The A string fingering is the same as that used on the G and D strings.

MELODY

Grazioso

MARCH IN D

Moderato

The D and A strings

Play the D string tetrachord followed by that of the A string and the result is the SCALE OF G MAJOR.

Practise also with 2 and 4 notes per bow.

G major arpeggio

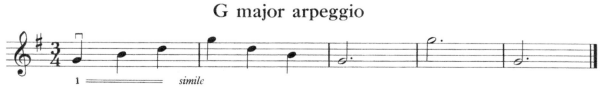

Practise also using a bow to each bar.

KATHLEEN'S WEDDING

CHATTERBOX

Easy Position Tunes for Viola

The C string

Keep your left elbow tucked under the viola and allow the thumb to slide under the neck of the instrument. This will ensure a good left hand position and correct finger action.

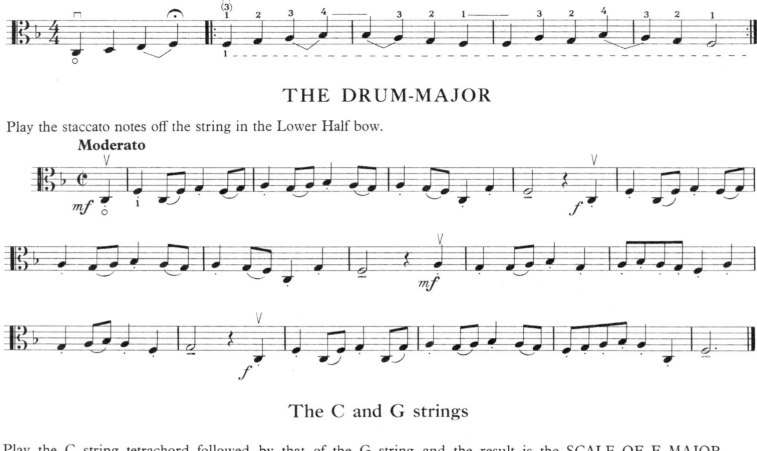

THE DRUM-MAJOR

Play the staccato notes off the string in the Lower Half bow.

The C and G strings

Play the C string tetrachord followed by that of the G string and the result is the SCALE OF F MAJOR.

Practise also with 2 and 4 notes per bow.

F major arpeggio

Practise also using a bow to each bar.

MINUET

GAVOTTE

Tempo di gavotta

2nd POSITION

The D string

Pause on the note F, then move the hand up to 2nd position so that the same note is played with the first finger.

PADDY McFANE

Allegro

The last note is an Artificial Harmonic. Press firmly with the first finger on F, and lightly with the 4th on B♭. This should produce a sound two octaves above the stopped note F.

A KELTIC LAMENT

Andante

The G string

The G string fingering is the same as that used on the D string.

THE WATER WHEEL

Allegretto

HIGH TIME

Tempo comodo

The G and D strings

Play the G string tetrachord followed by that of the D string and the result is the SCALE OF B♭ MAJOR.

Practise also with 2 and 4 notes per bow.

B♭ major arpeggio

Practise also using a bow to each bar.

Easy Position Tunes for Viola

COUNT BRONOWSKI

IAN FINDLAY'S REEL

The A string

The A string fingering is the same as that used on the D and G strings.

THE FALLS O' FEARN

SONG OF STORNAWAY

The D and A strings

Play the D string tetrachord followed by that of the A string and the result is the SCALE OF F MAJOR.

Practise also with 2 and 4 notes per bow.

F major arpeggio

Practise also using a bow to each bar.

NEGRO SPIRITUAL

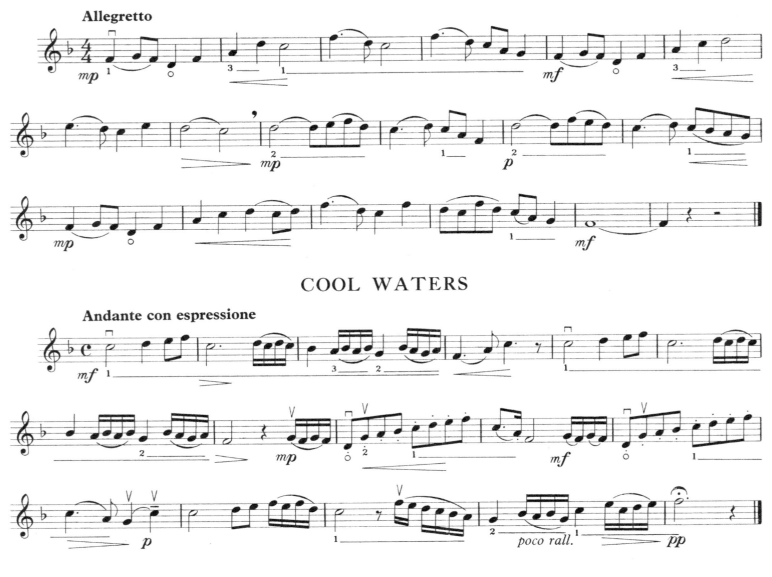

COOL WATERS

The C string

The C string fingering is the same as that used on the other three strings.

REGRETS

The C and G strings

Play the C string tetrachord followed by that of the G string and the result is the SCALE OF E♭ MAJOR.

Practise also with 2 and 4 notes per bow.

E♭ major arpeggio

Practise also using a bow to each bar.

FANTASIE

Processed and printed by
Halstan & Co. Ltd., Amersham, Bucks., England

OXFORD UNIVERSITY PRESS

ISBN 978-0-19-357651-3

OXFORD UNIVERSITY PRESS

EASY
POSITION
TUNES
FOR VIOLA

Exercises and Melodies
for class and individual use

NEIL MACKAY

NOTE

This book is a simple introduction to playing in 3rd and 2nd positions and does not deal with changing position.

The finger patterns throughout are built on the tetrachord system (tone, tone, semitone) and so the 4th finger is close to the 3rd when in use. This makes it easier for the student to use the little finger and should help to strengthen it without stretching along the fingerboard.

Phrases are punctuated by commas or rests and the tunes have been carefully edited so that students may improve their musicianship by observing these musical details.

Neil Mackay